EMOTIONAL TRENDZ

EMOTIONAL TRENDZ

ROMEO WEEPING

Order this book online at www.trafford.com
or email orders@trafford.com

Most Trafford titles are also available at major online book retailers.

Printed in the United States of America.

ISBN: 978-1-4907-3690-7 (sc)
ISBN: 978-1-4907-3692-1 (hc)
ISBN: 978-1-4907-3691-4 (e)

Library of Congress Control Number: 2014909159

Illustrations/Sketches by **Tim Morgan**
Cover Photo by **Shaina Olsen**

Trafford rev. 05/30/2014

 www.trafford.com

North America & international
toll-free: 1 888 232 4444 (USA & Canada)
fax: 812 355 4082

*Dedicated to my God, my wife and my best friend
for which may not always comprehend my insanity
but has always been there with open arms.*

Preface

Emotional Trendz is a lifetime of uncertainty for Romeo Weeping. A tuff gruff style exemplifies a courageous man with a gifted mission. Romeo Weeping lives in the transition of everyday life. He is no more capable of controlling his emotions than he is driven to write. The following represents a lifetime of thousands of literary pieces he has composed, it is here you will only begin to understand the why to Romeo Weeping. I would venture to guess that as much as we feel we understand this man, we are so very wrong. He writes not because he needs to, he writes to survive the turbulent world in which he attempts to understand. I'm not sure after meeting him and editing his work that I understand more than the simple fact that he is compelled to appreciate what little he has control of. In his own way he understands better than most of us, and shares this with an honesty some people would just refuse to accept. I hope that he writes forever.

Anthony Trupiano

Enter Emotional Trendz

I've invited you into my world to see
but I warn you don't fall in too deep
for you may slip inside and fall
and yearn to never leave at all
You can pick through the shadows and take what you will
then turn away when you've had your fill
Your host is a fair man it's your choice to go
My prison won't hold you this I already know
I only ask for small things I'm sure you'll see
each thought you may take but leave one for me
I'll make it a mountain for if you return
We'll climb to the top where we both can learn
I'll tell you how it looked to me
You're free to come and go as you please
If your heart is strong i think we can begin
step into my world of . . .
Emotional Trendz

The Beast And The Butterfly

One day a butterfly beautiful as can be
chanced upon a beast leaning against a tree
the butterfly flew away in fright
to flee from the awful sight
Then the butterfly heard his plea
please don't go stay here with me
Something in his grotesque voice made the butterfly slow his pace
and turned to look upon his face
Distorted it was to his surprise
tears flowed from his eyes
the butterfly landed upon his breast
and asked why are you sad what causes this sadness
the beast then said of all my days
I've been a beast and I'm tired of this way
I want you to help me feel your beauty my friend butterfly
the butterfly then said you can't help what you are
but I'll tell you something that may get you far
When you look upon your face
don't look upon it with distaste
Before you can accept what you may be
You have to accept yourself and pull shame free
and listen to this a little more
to change yourself is up to you that's what dreams are for
So now they are the best of friends
Can you find the moral, I hope so
The End

The Conductor

Out of the shadows emerges
The conductor
the curtain ascends
He drains the room of whispers
tapping the baton against the podium
His heart skips a beat
as I bring the multitudes together as one
unpure hearts shall not pass
his eyes blur by sight of sound
a split second before the crowd
hears the first note
from his fingertips it becomes . . .
The art of breaking silence
with a slight stroke of a hand
slicing the air from within
from silence to sound
dark becomes lite
As a fire burns within
as he gives them life
the crash of the cymbals
the soft strokes of a string
or the whispers of winds
first comes from he
The heartbeats blend with the tempo
entwined in a heated passion
the whole room breathes as one
introducing the final note
arms raised head bowed
The sparks become a twinkling ember
the curtain descends
leaving them awed and overwhelmed
there is no final note
For the conductor lives forever in symphony

A Poem

You
were love
that could be so warm
and cold
and painful
and crushing
I
enjoyed your pain
looked for it to come willingly
tried to understand it was no more
We
loved once
we were happy together
it ended too soon for me anyway
Life
is just as good as death
only a lot more painful
that it numbed my heart
Deaths
saber is so sharp
but the sword of life
is double edged and dull
Pain
yes every minute
second hour day
year decade
century
Love
has no time for me

A Moment In Pain

The head is pounding
the chest is tight
the stomach groaning
there is no lite
the heart is broken
you've won the game
my mind is shattered
I'm going insane
my life is nowhere
nothing is good
trying to fake it
like I know I should
I'm drowning in tears
and I don't know why
hiding the pain
stiffening the cries
days are o.k. there's always distractions
the nites have more shadows
the darkness is no more satisfaction

The Legend Of "Never Will Be"

This morning I woke from a restless sleep
blindly I walked out into the street
I was caught in a rush of anonymous faces
people rushing off to unknown places
I suddenly realized the piercing cold
the question unanswered I stood alone
I asked an old man who slowly walked past
where am I sir? or may I ask?
he said you're confused its plain to see
but you're in the land of Never Will Be
then I pleaded "please explain"
we walked into the café to get out of the rain
he said it's a long tale to tell
but I'll make it short, so listen well
everything here is not as it seems
it's not real, it's in your dreams
I thanked him for his time
to pay for his coffee I threw a dime
i walked to my bed and lay back down
I'm happy now for what I've found
because while there I did not see
you, my love in Never Will Be

On Never Will Be

Regret not our Never Will Be
seek only your deepest desires
real life could Never Be
the same as your inner fire
Never pain those dreams you seek
they will always live here with me
no matter how you say goodbye
you will never hear me cry
however far you seem to be
Regret not for what will Never Be
a gypsy like love I never knew
though I stay here to play that fool
I regret no more for Never Will Be
it's not my pain to bare
You are always in the dreams i seek
though you no longer see me there

Lost Poems

Unsung songs I've yet to write
lay hiding in my mind
shadows that keep me awake at nite
scared to close my eyes
should a dream come that I can't remember
or should you have a poem
in my mind it could get lost forever
a poem that has no home
for each poem has touched someone
and is remembered in their mind
there the poem has found its place
forever in that mind
could one cry for a poem now lost
or dreams that may fail
i can for the love of poetry songs
isn't that all

M.I.A.

I stared into the glass, hypnotized
more in awe than transfixed
the eyes that I saw there were the same shade of my own
only many years aged
I saw hatred, envy and rage
sorrow guilt and pain
beneath it all, I saw loneliness
not a loneliness for another's touch
a smile, a voice or a supporting crutch
I yearned for an unnamed thing
perhaps something I never had known,
though it was something missing
I dare to guess what it may be
but it's not in me
loneliness it was and today still is
it's the only name I can give it
I've learned to live with that vacancy
better than i had so many years before
Missing In Action

Mass Confusion

Chosen ones so often die, the old legends say
hero's lie within graveyard fences, or damn near on their way
tears in every life must fall
every soul has touched some pain
nitemares have found more innocent minds
than lives thrown down the drain
this i call mass confusion
a distortion to the eye
There is only one question i ponder
who is he, that makes all cry?

Misery

Misery loves company
though I make mine alone
and later maybe then I'll tell
but why not bury those old bones
misery will always come
till all the sins are paid
so if misery wants company
i guess it'll just have to wait
why shake the shadows and tell
no cure can be found for this
my misery stands alone for now
but i know they can't resist
i accepted how things will be
no need to dig up those old bones
your misery may need company
but i prefer to keep mine alone

Toy Box World

Toy box world something like these days
but in every young childhood, where lives are only for play
we set up our playthings to live like pretend
while grooming our minds in "Emotional Trendz"
dreaming "I love you's" is the cure for world peace
growing older and realizing you still believe
faith for adventures are the games you once played
and the thirst for life's vigor is now a serious game
and just like the toy box that did fall
mending by imagination brought them back after all
and as the years go by we still dream and pretend
thus your never quite off of that "Emotional Trend"
going everywhere to find you go nowhere at last
because your memories always bring the Toy Box World back

Another Story For Explaining Love

Two bodies lay side by side
naked to the elements, they move not to hide
but to lie embraced not in body but mind
searching for answers sure not to find
emotions and feelings out of bodies they run
and fuse together until becoming one
pulled to each other by a force from above
these two bodies they've found love
a love spawned from heavens gate
and appointed path to each one's fate

Now two bodies lay side by side
fearing their fate, they run to hide
away in a corner they run to stay
they missed their love now bodies must stray
they look for their perfect affair
but wherever they look their love is not there
two bodies now must pay for the price of a non-commitment
till their dying day
now tell me, of these two pairs
which one are we?

The Waiting Room

Quite uncozy this silent room
no matter how many comforts they place here
nothing seems to brighten the picture
on the purpose for which i'm here
that grew inside over the years
can't help but feel the pain
though its been close to a year
i sacrifice my honor
every belief, a part of my soul
to give someone else happiness
separating the legal binds
but the truth is this
no matter what is done here on paper
no matter what i do to forget the binds that tie
that piece to me only gets tighter
i can't divorce that yet

Words of Wise

Dazzle your life with adventure and motion
stay strong to your heart to this lay devotion
keep guard on your pride for many men fall
stay alert when love arrives knocking at your door
dont give any less than you expect to receive
turn not one stranger away not all will deceive
walk lightly when you tread near someone's trust
this advice i didnt know but tell it i must
show not a face of anger but understanding when its hard
show more affection even when your tired
cross not a soul always keep a friend
be mostly true to your heart and you'll always win

Tomorrow's Yesterdays

The future is only somthing expected
its's never here so often neglected
Tomorrows are something to think about in dreams
to live for tomorrow is to dream
yesterday's something tomorrow's can never change
today's are for living to the full extent
for all todays are given to the major events

Between The Lines

Skipping in and out of reality and illusion
Doubting from within the terror and confusion
re-thinking steps to walk a new way
trying to face myself what can i say?
I see the headlines i know your gone, its on the wall everyday
how can i believe their all wrong?
what holds me back from letting go?
how much pain will i go through?
I guess time will bring it to me soon
I cant go on much longer
I lose sight more each day
slipping in and out between reality to insane

Temporary Love

Take my hand and come with me
enter into a land that no one sees
its a world you rarely find
with bright blue oceans and clear sunshine
before i unveil this place
look at me a while and feel my face
you've got to learn not to go so fast
let your emotions take over
i've been hurt in the past
now you understand my ways
come home with me and you'll see what i crave
it's your body your love and your style
even if its just for a while
I can live knowing i'll never have all of you
it would be usless to go on without the truth
so what was it we had
or what we thought
all this wasn't bad
look what it brought
something that is felt by few
it was a **Temporary Love** i had for you

My Prayer

Now i lay me down to sleep
praying i can have you in my dreams
seeing the eyes you loved me with
holding you close, this God's gift
walking together, hands held tight
showing each other loves delight
two people so close, almost as one
sharing each moment with laughter and fun
I pray that God hold's you when im gone
I hope for forgiving for all that was wrong
God so loved us He let us find out
life together forever is what it's all about
now i lay myself to sleep
where ever you are please dream of me
being alone is not His way
so He gave me your heart, hoping it would stay

What is Loneliness

Loneliness will find you
it chooses no color, no race and makes no appointment
loneliness has no mercy
it stalks those who are feeble, unsure and weak
then strikes without malice drawing from the most farfetched fear
and magnifying it ten thousand fold
loneliness is often mistaken as an unexplainable emotion
such as emptiness a feeling of missing something
a yearning in the pit of your stomach
but is stll yet unknown
and no one is safe from its wrath
rich, poor, happy, satisfied or unsure
everyone has that loneliness

Time Piece

Time is just a healer, a piece of memory
time is just a stealer, from age and history
time is but a marker for distant memories
time is for believers, just like you and me
time is but an hour, where minutes gather to make
time is something we all have to give or to take
time is your friend, your enemy, we still all have time to see
time will make it all come true, dreams and fantasy
and when it comes in each of us, where time is spent and gone
time always leaves us memories our young can carry on
time is all but easy, no time can cure all wrong
this world can seem so empty
without time to carry on

My Color Is Black

Black is my color it's always been
I call shadows my home and feel death a good friend
Love is my enemy, pain is what i most know
for black is my color deep in my soul
bars out of teardrops i made my own prison
will i ever get past them, won't someone listen
black is my color don't you agree
though many have tried they won't change me
despair is my mother, my father is sin
mix in the evil you may understand where i've been
don't try to save me i like it this way
with black is my color i know you wont stay
for the pit is my desire don't throw yourself in
you'll feel you got lucky but you'll burn here within
don't try to love me i can't give it back
my life lies in shadows
My Color Is Black

Paper Wall Prison

Sitting here in my paper wall prison
the pain in my heart is ripe and seasond
stop and listen to the trees
they speak of love as they sway in the breeze
i heard your voice just then
i know it traveled on the wind
i know not what was said
still i'm not sure . . . . it was you in my head
it doesn't matter why i'm here
i was locked in here by you
upon your return my sentence is through
will you return to let me out?
or is my future already spent
my whole life on this payment?

She

She's been through heartache's, she's been hurt alot
i've picked her up at times, hey she's all i got
she's shared a lot of dreams with me, even made a few
she could sing a ballad and pick me up whenever i felt blue
we've been through a lot of cities, seen alot of ladies let me down
each time i've been shut out, she's always been around
i've held her body and cried all nite, when only she could hear
it's always made my life so fine, whenever she was near
she's been the best partner, who always helped me sing
if i ever needed to be loved, she'd give me anything
she's perfection in her own way, but i see it too
she's been my only true love, it'll never be through
it's been o.k. to be in love, she's the only apple of my eye
if she ever really made me blue, i really needed to cry
at times when i've been so angry, i've almost
put my fingers through her neck
she doesn't mind i get it out, and i havent hurt her yet
yes you can say i'm in love, i'll always be
if you ask me what her name is, it's rainbow to me
i know your probably really confused so far
if you think i've been talking about my girl
i havn't i've been speaking of my guitar

~ 25 ~

Green Grass

Grass always grows greener on the other side
but nothing has changed though you thought it might
each thing you grow tired of doing nite and day
have you looking to what seems like a better way
but you don't see while you're trying so hard to hide
there are people watching the grass that grows on your side
till you finally choose and go over that fence
where the grass grew much taller, and what happens next
you realize you left behind things you can't do without
but then it's too late to return anyhow
the grass you left behind now someone else tends
and the fence you jumped over has no gate to come in
the doorway back is often not found
you must now tend the new grass and the fence you tore down
the grass now dies and withers away
will the teardrops in spring bring them back in May?
are the weeds and thorn patches choking so hard
that you can't see the grass growing in your yard
pull them away let that grass break through
the grass will always be greener on your side too

God's Talk

Dear God, it's me again
could you lend and ear this way?
i know it's been a while
since you and i have had much to say
i have a question i need to know
it burns me lately, down in my soul
i'm young and beginning to be a man
so tell me, am i going to make it?
do you think i can?
will everything be alright tomorrow
or shall i drown in my own tears?
i want to know if everything will change
or will i be a victim of my own fears?
as these words had fallen from my mind
i lay there and a voice whispered softly to me in rhyme
"my dear child i've heard your pen
i have answers if you'll listen to them
as you've suffered i've also cried
for in your heart i have tried
each time i've told you trust in me
for in the end you will be free
each time i've tried to show you more
you stayed alone behind closed doors"
It was selfish of me, i know that now
to hide under a cloud
saving myself, and only He knows
He's always been there and that's how it goes
you realize your fears shoud not be
trust in your heart, He said to me
the silence that fills the void where He'd been
left me with a peace and a place to begin
i should remember more often than i do
only one fear will harm, that fear is of You

I Dealt The Devil

I dealt the devil in a poker game
only to gain fortune and fame
but i dealt the devil just the same
and now i must live with this shame
he shuffled the deck, a master of cards
while behind him stood his evil guards
he dealt the cards one by one
till five were laid then he was done
i had three kings with an ace to kick
but the devil pulled off with a royal flush trick
i knew right then that i'd been beat
but i had the suspicion the devil had cheat
so i threw down the cards, looked him in the face
you're a cheater, i screamed in rage
his grin said that i was right
you should know better than to play with me at nite
then his guards grabbed me and down i fell
and i knew then i was bound for hell
all i could do then was scream
that woke me from my dream
yes a dream of fear and pain
just a dream but all the same
i wonder when i die where i'll be
if it's going to be heaven or hell for me?

Social Survivors

Ain't we something one of a kind
just social survivors, ruler's of our minds
putting dreams into thoughts one can never be sure
where reality ends, comes forth a cure
to share a thought, it's the way we know
to spread a dream and make it grow
yes, we're the little middle people
they all over looked
we are the peaceful soldiers
giving back what time took
we are the hands that hold every heart close
the memory of some, the promise of none
we just want what they want most
step inside what we all dream
what we see is how far we go
we will be as far as we believe
and ain't we something, just many of your kind
social survivors, the rulers of our minds

Endless Dream Called Believing

There's a man who's not sure
of where lies a cure
in his endless dream called believing
when his love takes a walk
and there's no time to talk
don't you want to know what he's thinking
well i can tell that it's true
of what he's going through
in his endless dream called believing
yes there are too many ways to forget her
but he's not sure
which road will take him home
so mister try it all now
for it's the only way how
or you're forever sure to roam
and as he's shaking off the cold
his head is about to explode
yes that's the lady that he used to know
who left him sitting in the cold
hopelessly wasted and turning old
and he's living in his
Endless Dream Called Believing

Field Of Time

How could you really share this dream
they may judge you and find you extreme
they'll never know the field of time
where memories and images rode on by
you gun the throttle for the final race
cross the field of time, none to waste
racing so long your muscles race and tremble
so close to the finish you let off the throttle
thinking you're even seeing this in your mind
then comes another racer not far behind
you both gun down for the final turn
your fears reignited . . . you both take the curve
side by side, no one gaining a bit
you both loose traction as you pass the pit
your wheels entangled as you cross the line
going down in metal, what did you find
as your eyes met his and before you awoke
came the smell of raw gas and the clearing of smoke
your heart dropped and your veins turned to ice
for their stood your twin staring back in your eyes
i couldn't tell you my friend, i could only ponder the meaning
for in my dreams always lie a different meaning
i've heard if you struggle in the end it never comes
in the field of time there isn't one

Average Anxiety

Anxiety i would say
is not something you can hide away
it shows no matter where you are
anxiety can't be hidden in a jar
unless of course you are unlucky
to have less than average anxiety
anxieties are society's dreams and hopes
they help you in life they help you cope
i will always have a dream you see
because i have more than average anxiety
if you are unhappy i wish for you
at least a little anxiety too

Blues Singer

There was an old man sitting in the rain, no place to go
sits there playing guitar, catching dimes that people throw
singing the blues is all that he'll ever know of his life
lost three kids in a hurricane and a trucker took his wife
no matter how hard he tries, he can't push the memories out
when he sings the tunes of sorrow, his voice cries right out
so emotions draw a crowd
and tears drop from his eyes as he sings out loud
he lives in a shack at the far edge of town
and just like his life, its run down
this man has the power to make people see
he showed the world what he can be
in his younger days he could have been a star
he could have had fame near or far
but now he sings depression, he ought to know
catching dimes people throw
he can live with the blues, anyone can
i ought to know because i am the old man
and my future is what ive been telling you
its what i see, nothing i can do
ill write sad songs and prepare for the day
that i sing them to passers-by
who throw change and walk away

Just A Thought

What is in my heart now matches the things that i hoped for
nothing
i feel i can only grow when im in your presence
but
i grow tired, hopeless, hurt and lonely
why
it has come to a point where trust has gone from everything
too empty
why am i sorry for my life
don't know

For My Chlidren

I fear for my children for what they will see
i fear for their future and what they believe
i fear that some army will take them away
for some poor excuse backing the american way
i fear for my children and what they now know
i fear that they'll never see children of their very own
i fear they'll never remember bushes forest or trees
and that the world will run out of all it's good things
i fear for the children who starve today
i fear that tomorrow that mine just may
i fear that their innocence to soon will be gone
in this mixed up world i've lived this long
i fear each nite when i tuck them in bed
that tomorrow wont come for these children i've bred
i fear that they lost things they never had
i fear for them most because i'm their dad

Can You Be With Me Tonite

Can i still have you when i'm dreaming?
can you let me have you there?
can i place you in my love songs?
will you be my lover there?
when i close my eyes tonite
will you be closing that door again?
you left my life so long ago
my dreams having you leaving again and again
can i kiss you under full moon's
in my candy coated dream life?
won't you let your soul be there with me
when i close my eyes tonite?
can i still dream of you my love?
will you still let this be?
tonite when you close your eyes
will your heart be here with me?
can i still hold you in my arms?
only you can say
will you come to my dreams tonite
till the dawn takes you away?
can you see me there in your illusions?
i can always see you in mine
can you be with me tonite?
even if it's the last time?

Grandfather

When i was young i sat on his knee
hours of stories he told to me
with distinguished grey hair and eyes of stone
now he's old and i'm near grown
my father left home when i was a lad
but grandpa was there and all i had
he rarely asked for anything
only love which wasn't hard to bring
by all right's i'd say he's perfect
in my eyes anyway, he sets
not even my father can take his place
no one is even in the race
as much as i feel my love for him grow
i feel i never let him know
isnt that the way it always is
he know's the lite in my eyes is love when mine meet his

Let It Be

Some say your no good for me
you'll pick me up in time of need
play around with my mind
setting me down when you don't have time
you'll tear my heart up to see what you've found
while telling the world im your clown
i say to them, let it be
you've been around so long you're a part of me
pick me up once more i'll be your toy
I can play the game i have all along
each time i play i get a little more strong
when i no longer have to strain
to smile and show i have no pain
people will say you're going to tear my world apart
i say let it be, i'll show you where to start
don't worry about it, i won't even shout
take my heart and rip it out
step on it hard, crush it into the ground
don't pitty me, just turn around
walk away, don't ever look back
don't listen for my heart to crack
i play the game, but the rules aren't fair
you inflict your pain, now realizing where
you can't see what's behind these eyes
you never hear the people criticize
when they tell me that you're treating me bad
and our love is just a long gone fad
i'll say to them you'll never stop caring
when we still have our times for sharing
who the hell cares? it's not up to me
and i just say
Let it Be

At The Carnival

Popsicles, candy apples, pony rides and carousels
bright lites under starry nites, jingling of the bells
remember how it seemed back then when games were played for fun
just like them we grew so fast, tore it down and then were gone
old pieces now remain laying on the ground
for someone to sweep away, pick up and carry on
AFTER THE GOOD TIMES

Ode To John Lennon

Remember his songs, i remember them well
for in each lies a story to tell
remember the sad December day
when a bullet took our idol away
that was the day we all cried
on a cold winter day John Lennon and the music died
we can't bring him back this martyr of a man
only remember he was loyal to his fans
he stood for love and peace on earth
never did he lose sight, what was it worth
he wrote the songs that made us dance
please carry this message
Give Peace A Chance

A Letter From Lennon

If they could only hear my message man
if they could only see
what i was trying to tell them
before the bullets caught up with me
you gotta love your neighbor
go on and take his hand
tell him just how much you care
are you willing to take a stand,
to find eternal peace
is all this world needs
come on people
get up off your knees
oh how i wish i could have seen
the peace before i died
i had one shot at it
and oh, how i tried
wake up and realize my dream could come true
sure it needs sometime and a little help from you
can't you see man love is on your side
it's there for the taking no rules to abide
but who now will carry my tune
who could fill my space
who has the courage and the heart
to reach all the human race
mostly who is worthy to take my dream
who could endure that much pain
i only hope he knows who he is
and the odds against this chore

to hold wisdom when his back is against the wall
only he could find the door
for now we fight for no real gain
and the world hungers for love
but all there is to feel is pain
so this is my letter
please see that the people share it
for i'll not be gone in this world
i'll be here for you in spirit

The Man

Sheets of music
words wrote down
i entered his room
without a sound
his pen lay still
the desk was cluttered
felling him still
i suddenly shuddered
what had he been saying
when i saw him last
what did the note say
about his past
put the records back on
set the mood
sat down in the place
he called his room
lifting his pen
i glanced at his notes
picking up at the place
that he last wrote
then the word came back
i saw suddenly
i was in my own room
yes i was he

Ain't It Funny

In a dark cafe south of L.A.
sit's a woman with memories of yesterday
thinking of better times in the past
hoping each day will be her last
ain't it funny how time can't ease the pain
even when the memories somehow fade
you awake and the world has passedf you by
ain't it a shame when all you do is cry
she tells her stories to all who will lend an ear
of a wild free past, choking back the tears
when a man promised fortune and fame
said the lites of broadway would bare her name
how was she to know it was only a line
her dream was shattered in his good time
and in the morning to her trusting eye
she found herself in a bed made of lies
now she sits alone in a dark bar room
listening to a country band way out of tune
drinking beer and singing along
trying to figure out a love gone wrong

Darker Than Black

In your mind . . . sometimers
a shadow can seem darker than black
I close my eyes sometimes to escape
and once the blackness subsides
my mind becomes a playground of colors
reds that are so vivid i can see it spill onto an empty canvas
mixing in with the velvety blues
and whites that seem to seperate all these
a thin wisp of eveness . . . is white
so that one does not contrast with the others impressions
if the world outside could only be
where no image outshines another
where each different shade compliments the outside edge of another
if we could all be
like i see
in my mind . . . sometimes
when its
Darker Than Black

For John {Bonzo} Bonham

Hey Bonzo, where'd you go?
I bought the tickets and you stopped the show
took a ride to the promise land
buried you with drum sticks in hand
through the Ocean and Dyer Maker you beat on your drums
and there was no guitar for you
yes, you're through
so high, you were so high you died
but dont feel sad i didn't cry
even though there will be another
a new drummer will come
but why should they bother?
old Zepplin the greatest they'll ever be
but the boys are all old
and you're already free
hey Bonzo, where'd you go
i had the tickets
and you stopped the show

Philsophy Of Miss Jane Pittman

There was a woman of a hundred and ten
who realized her life would shortly end
when asked the secret of longeveity
she tapped her cane against an old oak tree
now others she said would think it's not right
to talk to this tree, as i might
but for twenty years it's been my fashion
to talk to the trees the way i've been accustomed
the oak tree stands tall with nobility
not as tall as an apple or spruce could be
oh, Miss Jane Pittman was her name
who looked with death without any pain
and on a day some still recall
a time she walked and stood so tall
up a sidewalk to a fountain of water
forbidden to her, but still she sauntered
took a taste of the water, caught every eye
Miss Jane, she had all surprised
her dream of peace spurrred this on
the years of pain gone, pride made her strong
turned and smiled toward the white man
announced herself, Miss Jane Pittman
and after here show of mobility
Miss Jane toasted to that old tree
had it not been for the tree she spoke
i would have not made it if not for the oak

Mommy Please

My little girl is four years old, she puts the sparkle in my eyes
my young man though he's just a boy, he helps me to get by
these two young people are my world, what
can i say when i hear them cry
mommy mommy please come home, don't you know we miss you so
daddy hide's but we still know
because we hear his cries, he's so alone
mommy won't you please come home
oh, they're both so sweet, she has her eyes
and just like me there's alot he hides
most time's they're happy or at least you know they try
but it hurts me so to hear them cry
mommy mommy won't you please come home
we pray each nite you will
daddy says you won't love him again
though he loves you so much still
momma we need you to watch us grow
mommy please come home today
daddy won't smile anymore and he won't come out to play
he sits alone behind closed doors, looking at pictures of you
mommy come home and please make it soon
i can't tell them now, why their home is filled with tears
but i see they know it in their eyes
for they show much older than their years
they're being grabbed from childhood like
it happened to me so long ago
the only thing i can do for them is always let them know
my babies come let daddy hold you, i'll never leave you alone

i know you love her but understand mommy can't come home
her heart has told her she can't stay
and too soon you'll do the same
daddy's the one who will always cry about the way that things became
remember daddy loves you both and mommy surely love you
i promise i'll be here and it's alright, because i miss mommy too
i miss her too

Dedicated as song to Steve B.

Rebel Rider

Dressed up to raise hell, leather and chains
high heeled boots and gold diamond rings
a silver braided necklace wrapped around my neck
with the cross of Jesus to keep the devil off my back
yeah, dressed up to raise hell, with no place to go
dark shades, tattoos and a heavy bank roll
what's to do now, dont think i could face the day
when i stand at my window, looking at the rain
coming down from the heavens like a burial shroud
there aint no remembering the pain as long as the music's loud
dressed up to raise hell, so that's what i'll do
forget the clouds outside cause i'm gonna find you
you'll hear my motor racing outside your door
throw on your cheap dress, you don't need momma no more
jump on the saddle and hold me tight
we're out to raise hell, and be gone all nite
don't try to stop me, the wheels must keep turning
dressed up to raise hell, bridges are burning
i'm not stopping till they lay me down
no sense of hoping of coming back now
dressed up to raise hell leather and chains
high heeled boots and gold diamond rings
silver braided necklace wrapped around my neck
running off to nowhere and never coming back

Dedicated as song to Steve B.

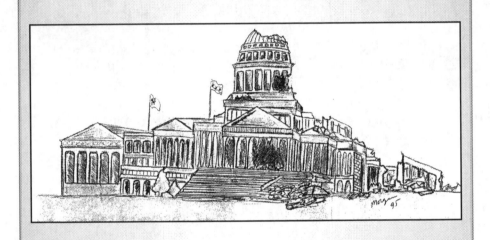

Political Madness

Wise men sit upon their thrones
casting down judgment like it was their own
taxing poor people that don't have a clue
political madness is all around you
how they forget the priomises that got them there
their deaf to our cries now they no longer care
while we wonder how to live or what next they'll do
what more will they take from me and you
as wise men sit upon their thrones
guiding our lives where they want them to go
stealing each penny we try to save
political madness is only their game
no one can guess where it will end
till the blood of the innocent spills once again
yes political madness has always ended this way
and it's the blind sheep like us who will pay
to give another wise man a chance for a change
while his pockets become deeper than the one he replaced
a new wise man will sit where others have been
*to start **Political Madness** all over again*

Heaven's Angel

When i find myself missing you
there's a fresh tear that hits the floor
i feel more and more i'll never make it through
everyday i miss you more
heaven's where my angel stays
they needed one more that i
can't see why they took her away
God, dont let them see me cry
girl, you think i'll forget you soon
but i'm so alone to even try
i still can't believe it's true
we never got to say goodbye
heavens where my baby stays
they needed one more angel there
how will i make it through lonely days
if my angel can't be here
Lord, don't let them tears fall again
i'm not that strong anymore
and every time im missing my angel
a fresh tear hits the floor
one day i know when i pass
my angel will be there for me
but now more than ever i need her so
i can't get used to being lonely

The Play Called, "Then You Died"

*My love was so empty i didn't know where to turn
she said she would never lite me up just to see me burn
i was the fool, yes, i was the dump-on for you
but tonite I have my vengence, something i have to do
when you sleep tonite, you will forever hear the sound
of your last dying breath as i hit the ground
i'll stalk your windows to see you dream of my love
i'll draw my gun and you'll never see it come
and seconds after the bullet has lodged in your brain
the last drop of blood will fall and i will be insane
i'll laugh a high pitch, who's even now?
as i snip my life out and the curtains come down*

Storms From Nowhere

Drowning in an ocean of emotion
sacred promises, dreams and such
i still feel that simple notion
those things are never enough
i see the storms roll in from nowhere
but i make all promises true
in the dark clouds, i'm happy to be here
i question if you still do
I've come from nowhere to be here
from darkness i came to lite
i find more comfort in the music of thunder
while the rains wash my spirit tonite
as the storms roll in from nowhere
my chances are that i'll feel them soon
where in this i still find the pleasure
but i wonder if it's still in you
and when the storms roll in from nowhere
i know i'll never run to hide
for inside their fearsome torment
no one has ever seen me cry
as the clouds rush in i turn to smile
here comes another one
i enjoy the thought it's just here for me
i mourn when their all gone
storms from nowhere will always scare you
but for me i've always been there
*walking in this rain . . . **Storms From Nowhere***

Emotional Trendz

Nite Lite's

My dream stands alone inside a world of many
my illusion is just an illusion inside a world of none.

Nite has cought me lying next to you
wondering why we've made up our minds what we'll now do
about love found, love lost and love
we'll always deny between us two

Due to the cause of non-conformance i will stand alone
no one cares, and they all run scared, when i do things on my own
now for the price of solitude, i'll let them have their own way
it's all because of me, what i'll be, not just for tomorrow, but today

Amongst the fantasy always lies fantasia
the difference between thinking and living your dreams

Part of the illusion is never what you see
pieces of a puzzle left out, you choose not to believe
it makes the job more complex than it really should be
for the master of illusion has never been me

Warm peace of being alone, not lonely, but not at home
a place where i can spread my wings and paste my ideas on the wall
a place of my own
solitude . . . in this noisy world

Where am i hiding? wont you come out and play?
it's so lonely playing by myself, life is just a game
where am i hiding? don't you wish to see?
come on out and find me, play hide and seek

If i were free careless as time
and i have for me any one thing for mine
to be alone in the rain in a silent retreat for me, this is fine

Baby, baby please don't cry
Tears should never touch thoese eyes
there is a reason your sad today although
in a future place those tears will go
you'll forget them as time goes by
there's an ocean of tears for those who cry

Hold me, show me
secure my trust
or leave me, believe me
if you think you must
it's o.k. by me, if its fine for you
i won't make a mess of your dreams too

It's o.k. if you hide your eyes behind your soft flowing hair
for i see them when i close mine

I only imagine how soft a touch could be
and how i'll feel when she touches me
not just once but a million ways in my dreams

Soft pink lips always say something different
than what the mind is thinking
they say so much more to a lonely soul

A common question we all ask is why the world is filled with shadows
though we run we will never hide
for there is no answers that we will ever find

The thing about love is that you cant hide it away
when its there no one could sway it to a place
where love doesnt want to be uncontrolled

My eyes are not yours, my mouth speaks not your words
my mind, though sharing, belongs to me
what i give you that is yours forever
is my love, friendship and honest devotion
but that is also mine

An ounce of trust
a heart of hope
one hand outstrectched
one lite touch
a dream wish answered
this is perfection
this is certain destiny

Can't erase the mind
will the mind ease the memories?
only the good one's leaving the bad
perhaps this is meant to happen

If you ever wondered and i know you do
will i need you forever?
no matter where or how far in the shadows you prefer
i will always need you

If the candle flickers do we put it out?
not unless when it was first lit was never meant to burn
starve a heart break, feed a love

If love isn't worth the fight for you
then for me it's not worth having at all

*You are
my wind
my fire
my one desire
my life
my love
my never enough*

*When happy things happen to me
i still look around to see
if you are standing somewhere maybe
around the corner, sharing them with me*

*If i am the person i want to be
and i don't know who i am now
how can i expect someone to be with me
if i'm going to change myself into someone i don't even know*

*A candle without a match to feed the inner soul, how can it burn?
kind of like love . . . agree?*

Be gentle
go easy
just love me, i'm still tender
no pain
whatever happens now in my life shall be good for me
looking at things this way shall carry me
all my life from now on
negative has no home here anymore

No more past eyes
no more past lies
the future is now, you'll do fine
i hope for no more pain nowhere
just peace
how could this ever be?
someone always cries

Always a memory or circumstances behind every written word
where do the memories go behind the wall?
what is left are the bare facts on the wall
how one felt or the memories of why
soon fade, lost forever, behind the wall

Seconds litening pasted me
hours run by
heartbeats grow louder
waiting for you

It's so hard anymore to know my personal self
i feel so much i thought was personal . . . but i shared them
was there a reason i haven't lost everything?
or am i just not seeing it?

Don't spend too much time on blame
mistakes unforgiven are probably bigger
errors than trying to remember
should have been things

If i said i love you, it wouldn't make any sense
after all the abuse, i'm trying to stay off that fence
and learn to tell myself, i love you

Tic, tock, time again
sitting all alone waiting for a friend
no one ever comes just the steady pulse of . . . tic, tock, time

You've hurt too long, too much to forget
could we be more than friends?
allow youself a chance to get there first

If you push to win, in a love once lost, you'll only do it wrong
if you leave it alone on its own it might come back

She keeps the same basic life pattern, but to those closest
unpredictable
woman

Carry a hope as if it were already there
need to hold on to something, hold on to your dreams

Fools so often come
fools so often go
but its fools like me when love is gone
realize how it hurt so

An ocean of pain separates our hearts
but a river of hope thinly runs through mine

Why can't i make your dreams come true?
when you're the center of mine

Love me for the person i want to be in my future
not the one i am now
but the one i dream i'll be

If your happiness can only be without me
this must come to pass
my only hope is someone, your twin, will make my dreams come true
and last, and last, and last, and last

Love will never catch me appreciating after it's gone
not next time, not anymore

The Gardner,
I would take any small piece of your heart if you gave it to me
i'd feed it with care, tenderness and hope, if I could just have a
seedling of kindness from you

Peace
peace is an elusive presence most search a lifetime to find
the secret of peace is you must find it in your mind first

Love
i don't think anybody is in love anymore, just sixteen-year olds
maturity takes away the magic part of love
making love- nothing but a vice or an addiction

About dreams
dreams that come true are rare and few
though nitemares are so many
i often look for them to show up in reality

Hearts
hearts are like captive eagles
once you set them free they won't survive recaptured

Lost and found
the more i lose, the stronger i am
the longer i go without, the farther i get
no ties, no binds
take it all from me
what i find is one thing
freedom

Easy things,
easy going, easy listening
easy rider, easy money
but easy life?
not in my book of themes

A Sunrise Without You

This morning i watched the sun come up
as the moon said goodbye
all i could do at the break of dawn
is sit alone and cry
a beautiful poem had struck me
of happiness to spare
and i sat alone and asked myself
man, why should you care
i had a chance to see with you
a daytime turned to nite
we never had our sunrise
never saw darkness turn to lite
it's the small things that make me realize
how little we truely shared
a sunrise here without you
my Little Miss Golden Hair

Dedicated as song to Steve B.

Dream Keeper

I am the dream keeper
please don't take that away
i put those dreams together
it's only right they should stay
they might be yours, but for now they are mine
i can't give them away, believe me i've tried
they always come back
i understand how they are
those dreams forgotten in time
in my mind they go far
yes, im the dream keeper
it's easy for me
only i have paid for them
i lost reality
here with me
i can make them at home
i am the dream keeper
i am never alone
it could never be done
to take them away
all that have tried
i've trapped in here to stay
very few of those will ever get out
i am the dream keeper
that's what im about

Dream Believer

Mister man please don't fold
don't despair or take my gold
give the people something they need
make a dream believer of me
change not a thing, keep my idea in mind
it took so much of me to find
mister man please don't despair
ask few questions, when i'm ready i'll share
keep faith as i have, they'll know my name
try not to hurt or cause me shame
the dream believer is not a man
it is my heart, do what you can
a friend once told me long ago
believe in dreams and make it so
i should have listened, so i guess
for now i'm a child taking first steps
try to vision every thought i see
and maybe you'll make a dream believer of me
if you can't do it for me, then how about you
are you a dream believer too?

Dream Seeker

I met the dream seeker
purely by chance
this dark eyed girl
showed me romance
it was surely unknown
how did she get in
i guess i didn't see the darkness
which lie hidden within
she the dream seeker
i felt i was too
i opened my heart
once again too soon
still looking for a dream
she'll never know
for always searching
she let me go
the seeker and the dreamer
wern't meant to be
that one i couldn't hold
no, not that dream
so fly little seeker
i'll let you go after all
you'll never be here again
i truely hope you don't fall
you are the one i should have never let in
but you are the one i released
go in peace if you can
i'll try not to hold my hate long for you

i've come to realize, it's what you had to do
yes, you'll be the haunting, that will forever be here
the reason no one will ever tread on my heart
no one will ever get near
goodbye dream seeker
i pray you don't fall
for you will never find your way
back over the wall

Dream Retriever

I once had a dream, it was mine no one shared
i once held a beauty, of one girl golden hair
though i couldn't keep it, the dream was so wrong
i wasn't ready for love, my heart wasn't so strong
i realized it would be better, just to let the dream go
in sadness she wondered, about things no one would know
i should have explained more, but i couldn't relieve her
it wasn't time to introduce, though i knew the dream retriever
it seems so right that she should be,
with someone so close
he could pick up the dream
no longer are they trapped, in my little dream poems
for life is so precious, i let them go on their own
now so much has passed, my heart flows different ways
i've known more of love, than in my younger days
the golden hair girl, and the retriever are free
the long ago pictures, are my memory
all this is fine, for we all have our place
they are all so certain, mine is still a maze
the dream is now faded, lost in time
the retriever holds what was once mine
so i only have myself to blame
so many dreams i once had
somehow thay have changed me
now i have a different world
torn and abused, by the dark haired girl

Magic Land

I was dreaming of a new love
on a cold and lonely nite
She was somehow familiar
for I didn't want to fight.
The Dark Eyed Girl said come take my hand
I'll show you a place
I call Magic Land
What was it I saw
that made me smile
I held her soft hand
she felt like a child
I tried not to care
but in Magic Land
I loved it there
She was right it was a magic place
I awoke in a start as my heart raced
How could I have ever known at that time
the Dark Eyed girl would be mine
Made from a dream I once had
My love forever in
Magic Land

Dream Singer

Who is the next chosen soul,
that carries the dream and surely knows
worthy to lead a dream others will follow?
the one who sees his time is now
the gold has already cast in his eyes
and his pure heart has told him it's time to fly
God has touched him once again
the dream singer now is "Emotional Trendz"
the higher you fly the more everyone knows
we are the gathers of the lost souls
world peace is our mission, a belief that we can
and the dream singers melody is in the plan
his magical music shall caress their ears
his soothing melody erase's all fears
coaxing the "Lamb's" back to the "Son"
dream singer you are surely the one
you're faith is far proven and now we are set to begin
join us now in this legion with
"Emotional Trendz"

Dedicated as song to Steve B.

Key Keeper

I hold the key that could expose many to the chance of a lifetime
i have my finger on the heartbeat of so many dreams yet unseen
though i've knocked on many doors
my key has yet to reveal a sliver of lite for them
i have this power building ever more
growing stronger each day
with each heart i embrace into the "Trend"
so comes the confidence to try each new corridor
my key will fit for them
and only in their sasisfaction
shall come mine

More Dreams (Dream Keeper)

Where do you keep them
where are they now
when the edges get frayed
do you still keep them around
dreams are so easy
dreams are free
but how is it very few people believe
pretty little pictures get painted in my mind
i have to give them away
before they become locked inside
i give them away because i'm never sure
if they are only my memory or someone else's cure
Dream Keeper just hold them
i know they'll be safe
maybe i'll need them again someday

Unsaid Things

Little white lies, better off unsaid
little lost loves, better off dead
what no one will know, then no one will pain
where no one speaks truth, in white lies friends remain
little black secrets forever unfound
are the unknown desires that lay buried deep down
little white lies forever unknown
should stay hidden for the hopeless if they're not just your own
little white lies all have their place
and illusion to carry or an impresion to make
a little white lie that will cushion the blow
to spare the pain of the innocent souls

Words Of Art

I paint a story only in pen it relieves my crowded soul
though you'll see the picture through your eyes
in a defferent way that i don't know
i color a field on paper here of greens and bright sunshine
you read a field of roses there then you have red on your mind
keeping the faith i've painted my way but in true your idea was there
and the dreams like yours will never fade on paper the place we share

Witches Brew

Have you ever heard the story of witches brew
it's got a saucy taste and it looks like stew
if you put it in your nose it'll singe the hairs
your eyes will bug out in a permanent stare
but if you really believe and you put it in your mouth
your tounge will tingle like it might come out
this brew was concocted by seven witches
to get a man right where he itches
and given to a lady named desire
with a heart of stone and a lust like fire
she catches men like me and you
hypnotizing with the witches brew
trapping their hearts in little glass jars
collecting their riches, promising stars
so watch out boys she has many faces
you'll see her in any hanging out places
it's hard to resist her and she know's its true
that's why she uses witches brew
i think everyday i'll escape her wrath
but i know i'll stumble into the path
for each man today is subject to
the captivation of
Witches Brew

Walls

*Walls resemble so much pain
so much sorrow so much rain
but sometimes walls can be your best friend
to be inside your mind to understand yourself within
look inside your mind you'll find you're not alone
the friendly walls are something that you'll always own
so my friend when i'm not there
and a problem arises you need to share
look inside yourself and then you'll see
something that the walls can't have
a little piece of me*

Up The Hill

Criticize
with all your lies
dress up the world
the way you will
keep in mind
what you'll find
when you reach the top of the hill
looking down
you'll hear the sound
of crying voices you made
then maybe you'll know
you prayed it would go
but the guilt will always stay
i say forgive
live and let live
you'll be judged on your own
and whatever you'll do
you'll answer too
when your mind won't let it go
there will be no blame
that won't carry your name
just live with what you've done
and i won't be there
to shoulder the despair
i must go on as one
don't worry for me
i still have a dream
and no more will they hide
those don't go away
and when i look back on my days
i know i took no one for a ride

Up The Hill

Time

All in a dream, all in lost time
did the numbers ever match?
was it a child-like rhyme?
will you ever trust again?
will you ever have a chance to dream?
you have got to realize that life's too short
so take it to the extreme
for what is your pen?
but a stroke of time
each second you wait
could lose you the ride
i've done this before and told you too late
the stroke of time was good for my fate
your luck may come in the course of time
but my friend you can't wait inside your mind
the seconds may catch you late once again
and your unforgiving mind has to let you begin
time that is lost is to never be found
so that a blink of an eye could turn it around
don't try to keep time with your destiny
for time here holds no currency
and waiting on time to begin a dream
is like waiting on a life that could Never Be

The Rope

As the fire eats the fine hairs of the hemp below
on this rope i cling to over the pit as each day passes
the slow fire takes more of the rope
when i started to wonder why i hang on
as my hands begin to glisten with sweat
the fighting for a hand makes my aching tendons scream in pain
for what worse could happen?
try so hard to keep my faith and not beg to show weakness
could it be for every good there is a counter part
if so i feel it could get worse
for i once new happiness so unbelievable that
maybe it was never real at all

The Writer

Give me a coke a pen and some paper a dream and bazooka gum
a little idea some faith and patience i'll sit here and write you a poem
a few cigarettes and some smiles later while we make a joke or two
when it's all over you'll wonder about me though
not as much as i wonder about you
you know i like walking through cemeteries
cause i feel the dead talk to me
dont think thats strange, i'll tell you now there i feel most comfortably
ok, so i'm a skittish outcast, but dont throw me no chains down
i'll show you a mind with so many surprises, you'll
never realize how much you've found
don't get sentimental, for im never sure if i ever give back enough
and i'll fill people's minds with so many illusions,
it's just my way dont like it? tuff
give me a coke a pen and some paper a dream and bazooka gum
a little idea and a few minutes later, i'll
hand you your own special poem

Magic Paper

I wish i was a piece of paper
one you could never throw away
a magic piece of paper
you could never fill up every space
thoughts that people tell me
they could write them down in rhyme
then if they ever needed to smile again
they could look to me anytime
i wish i was a magic piece of paper
that everyone could put their wishes on
and make them all come true for them
regardless if they were right or wrong
i'd be a sentence not erased from time,
but a thought that carries on forever
a magic piece of paper that holds,
every thought, dream or whatever

Paper Doll's

Paper doll's leave me alone
i can't play any more
i'm too far gone
super hero's, don't make me believe
i dress up this world just to make ends meat
fantasy, don't take me away
i went to often, i can't go again
money makes the world go round
so i'll shave my head to be their corporate clown
sweet innocence, your too long gone
as life's blood is drawn
away with the ages, this is me
taking with it dreams i once believed
paper dolls litter the floor
left behind i come no more
memories too soon fade away
don't wait for me, though i long to play
no time to dance or be with you
yet always know that i'll always want to
Paper Dolls

Short Thought

What can i say, pardon the intrusion
mastered confusion
living illusions
dreaming again
so close to insane
tired of the game
nothing stayed the same
if you look too long
you'll see it's wrong
but who is really where they belong
certainly not me
i don't see the same things
should i stay?
or go away?
i don't want to play
maybe tomorrow
but not today

Save For Daddy

A baby is born, daddy's at war
comes back a rich man his family stay's poor
yes daddy took a bullet but not a drop of blood was spilled
daddy only lost his mind on some black muddy hill
momma tried to save him said daddy still cared
but the boy grew up knowing daddy left his mind over there
when they all come home daddy tried so hard to make him see
he was not the hero that momma made him out to be
though he'd fought the war to him there was a bigger one
at home he'd catch the bullets the trigger would be pulled by his son
yes daddy took a bullet not a drop of blood was spilled
cause daddy only lost his mind there, he came home to be killed
who could place the blame on a child like mind inside the man
though the boy had never been there he too lost his mind in vietnam

Wishing Well

Wishing well here i stand
to ask a favor with a coin in hand
the wish i have to ask of thee
is to bring my lover back to me
she's been gone for such a long time
so please bring her back at the throw of this dime
many things ive tried thus far
from praying to God to wishing on stars
this alas was to no avail
at least can you tell me where i failed
i remember our walks by the sea
wishing well listen to me
or my heart will turn to stone
if forever i live alone

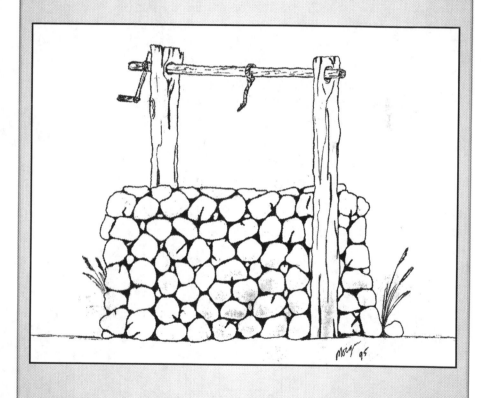

Coins In The Well

Copper clad coins in the wishing well, pennies stand as evidence
i wonder if mine are still there inside
for the dream has long since vanished
i thought the dream was once answered though in time it went astray
there was nothing i could do, just stand there
tear eyed as she walked away
and here i am again, coin in hand
without one dream in mind no wish to ask
no hope could last not for a lifetime
it occurs to me
i see a dream
a wish that will do
all these dreams
in the pool of themes
make them all come true

Spitting Images At The Well

You came asking the secret of the well
holding an empty cup for me to fill
silently watching the images spitting out
wondering so much what they're really about
parts of you and each person i see
is all my mind has left of reality
are you really sure you want to go
when the images are secrets you already know
the world is already cursed with little white lies
as for me you know all there is nothing more to hide
starting or stopping one never knows what to believe
and i won't color in your book of dreams
i already know the well that can quench your thirst
has to be found in your mind first
you'll see there is the perfect place for peace
my well can only have my soul to keep
for in the swirling waters below
spits out images even i didn't know
what you see in them i can't say
each eye will hold them a different way
the images you find are not always my own
your mind may be the only place they call home
if you think your strong enough to dare
come to my well, but tell no one you were there
you'll see the dream, but it's not mine
toss in the coin and close your eyes
let your spirit roam, go deeper still
the images will come if you let them spill
i doubt even now we're seeing the same

accept the peace, release the pain
the spitting images are not meant to hide
but the one's you fear stay trapped in your mind
once your in the well you'll beg to go home
but the images will never leave you alone
live it or wish it but never give up
on hopes and your dreams but mostly your love
keep true to your heart, make strong your will
you'll thirst no more for your cup is filled

Music Land

Have you ever been to music land
would you take a chance
do you think you can
there's lots of mysteries that you can't see
alot of secrets you'd like to know
we could walk up a Stairway To Heaven
to a House Called The Rising Sun
we'll meet a girl with Kaleidoscope Eyes
she'll teach us how to have so much fun
we'll ride a Yellow Submarine
alone Against The Wind
i'll let you know, i want you to be My Girl
and not just a simple friend
when darkness starts to enfold us
we'll watch the Lites Go Down In The City
and i'll whisper in your ear
I'll Be There any time you need me
that's not all in music land
but it's too much now to tell
this is only a land i've dreamed of
straight from the
Wishing Well

thanks to: Led Zepplin, Adam and his Ants, The Beatles,
Bob Seeger, Journey, The Temptations, Michael Jackson,
Eric Burton and The Animals and the Temptations

If I Died Today

A magical spell overtook me one day, there was nothing i could do
i walked out of my body in a peculiar way, do you believe it too?
well anyway i left my body, and in spirit i walked alone
i went to places i usually go, but no one knew i was around
someone said i was a drug addict, others said i was a theif
i heard everything bad about me things i couldn't believe
so i went back to my body, returned to my spirited soul
as i woke in a strange atmosphere, white lace around silver tent poles
my judgement day had somehow came, God
said you will be judged by your peers
i hoped that it was all a dream, my eyes filled with tears
God, i said i'm sorry, i didnt live my life your way
but things got harder in this world, since the time in Jesus day
i can't explain why i never turned to you,
when i knew it would be right
if i had all the faith, mabe i'd be alright
yes i've sinned and hurt a lot, and i can't tell you how it feels
to wake up and realize there's no hope, in today's people wheel
if there's no way i'm good enough for you,
let me walk down the low road
if it's what i must do
then he answered, but i never heard him speak
for i lay there thinking in my bed
did i die today?

Twas My Life As A Fish

I played a fish among the deep,
my survival was all but an ease
at first i could not digest the fact
i had to comsume my own kind to survive
this was a problem until i finally realized i had once been a human
our race has done the same
since time began
and very unlike what i had seen
i never attacked the weakend or from behind
much like my human side
i had swam in the sea of the cannibals
only to feast upon the feasting

Twas My Life As A Fish

My Pen And Me

If i have harmed your heart
or spoke unkind
may my words be gone
out of your mind
if i have turned your heart to stone
tis not my way
just so you know
my pen may harm your soul
in its scattered truth
but its only reflecting me
from age back to youth
so if you wail and have
teeth to grind
you've turned your eyes
to your own heart inside
it may have touched you
cut you or heal
only in your mind
but to me it's real
my only hope is that you see
what God has made of
My Pen And Me

Eulogy

Here lies the body of one man
a dreamer a poet a peace minded man
who once so loved the world his own way
but died lonely and heartbroken they say
no one could save him from the turmoil he had
who knows how much he would now have?
but he gave up and laid down and closed his eyes
tired of the pain and sleepless nites
so much he had in his mind for this world to give
but without her to share his dreams, could not live
no one else could hold him though many have tried
he was too scared to trust so he laid down and died
what justice he had ever hoped to see
he was one day short of having his dreams
for the girl swears now and each rocking day
that somehow she had tost track of what mistakes she had made
to late come apologies he's now in the ground
now no one knows where he is now
i can only believe heaven will take his soul
this was the eulogy of one Weeping Romeo

Just Throw Roses

I feel this should be mentioned before its my time to leave
when my eyes close forever just throw roses down for me
i don't know why i tell you but i feel someone should know
red, yellow, white ones too it makes no difference
but a single black one placed in my hands, i like them the best
this is the last gift ill except the one i'll never see
when i leave this world just throw roses then ill go in peace
it could have been to late to tell you if i hadn't thought of it tonite
so i wrote it down to let you know, if there
were no roses it wouldn't be right
roses are like my make up and i hope you understand
in my life roses didn't come easy, not for this man
i know black ones are rarely found but of course that's my best color
and red ones give me a kind of peace i could never find in another
i just thought you would like to know the
very last thing you can do for me
when you see them carry me away, just throw roses down for me

Judgment Day

Run for shelter if you can, judgment day is close at hand
don't trust anyone you know, the closest ones's will steal your soul
you can never hide the fear, the deamons are already here
watch the shadows where they creep, be careful where you fall asleep
they care not who they take, women and babies die each day
their bones shall rise from the ground, they'll
take your children without a sound
the devils saints shall sacrifice, the burning bodies will touch the sky
no where will peace find a home, each saved soul will stand alone
the fire will burn the world explodes, i should have told you long ago
you ran you hid you thought me insane, now
look around you and see it today
time is something no one will own, no rest
will come to the tortured soul
i can save you there's only one way, but
that's a chance you'll have to take
take my hand gather round, bring your loved one's hurry now
the stories i tell you take in your heart, leave your riches in the dark
hold on tight to my words, this may be the last time their heard
for Judas lies amongst us still, and prophesies must be filled
before they come to take me out, let me tell you what it's about
years ago when God made man, satan put evil in his left hand
it wasn't seen so much at all, but it grew so much within us all
people really didn't see what they were destroying,
the world could only take so much toying
the good disappeared day by day, and the bad
hand of lucifer was finally played
now with extincton in our time, put yourself inside your mind

let no one in think happiness there, try to
see harmony take a chance to care
inside your mind the devil can't take you, share
peace and show it in all that you do
leave hate at the door don't let him in. touch
all that you see think not of sin
perhaps we can't save them all, but for the sake
of the lost souls dont let them fall
the bad hand's deamon can't live in your mind, til
you open the door to just one of its kind
maybe we can save the world my friends, if
not you'll have peace until the end
remember my words and take them in
Judgement Day *is close at hand*

Victims Testimony

Heartbreak, pain, truth and pride
questions and answers no one can hide
fantasy, laughter, depression and fear
sands by the oceans filled with tears
hopes, dreams, rainbows and gold
roses and trendz, so the story is told
deep inside his mind
he can never let us go
even if he wrote it or told us so
is our choice really there to leave or to stay
i don't think it matters, he'll keep us anyway
a punishment to him, for a crime he's already paid for
inside him, he can't unlock the door
it wouldn't really matter if he gave the golden key
he would still have the nitemares and us the memories

About the Author

William F. Monroe was born on May 3, 1965 in Pontiac, Michigan. He is happily married to his loving wife Amy and has two wonderful children, Eric and Melesa, and five grandchildren. William moved to northern Florida in early 1974 and then back to Michigan in 1980. He attended Clarkston Senior High School, where he was a journalist on the school paper. He moved to Genesee County and graduated there.

William has had works published twice in the Poets Anthology and shares most of his works among his friends, family, and church. He was gifted several of his works pro bono to friends and family. William is very versatile, though works primarily in poetry and prose. He has been expanding into Hallmark style cards, short thoughts, lyrics, and short stories. He has worked with many artists; marrying his talents with theirs. He is currently working with Trafford to promote a lifetime of several books, all while balancing a full time management job.